D0246299

BA 0717 **132064** 9334

Leabharlanna Fhine Gall
BLANCHARDSTOWN LIBRARY
Inv/01 : 01/BA478 Price IR£10.25
Title: Remembered Kisses an
Class: REF 821.008

Remembered Kisses

*AN ILLUSTRATED ANTHOLOGY OF
IRISH LOVE POETRY*

Credits

Introduction Louis Bell

Editor Fleur Robertson

Designer Jill Coote

Jacket design Julie Smith

Production Ruth Arthur, Karen Staff,
  Neil Randles

Director of Production Gerald Hughes

Previous page:
A Ceilidh (detail)
School of William Mulready

Facing page:
Night (detail)
Sir William Orpen

4750: REMEMBERED KISSES

Originally published by Quadrillion Publishing Limited 1996.

Published in Ireland by
Gill & Macmillan Ltd, Hume Avenue, Park West, Dublin 12
with associated companies throughout the world.
www.gillmacmillan.ie

copyright © Salamander Books Limited, 2000

A member of the Chrysalis Group plc

All rights reserved. No part of this book may be reproduced, stored in
a retrieval system, or transmitted in any form or by any means,
electronic, mechanical, photocopying, recording, or otherwise, without
prior written permission from the copyright owner and Publisher.

ISBN 0 7171 3206 4

Printed and bound in China

Remembered Kisses

AN ILLUSTRATED ANTHOLOGY OF
IRISH LOVE POETRY

GILL & MACMILLAN

Coortin'
WILLIAM CONOR 1881-1968

Contents

Introduction

THE sheer exuberance and liberation of love seem to demand poetry. Lovers need a language that is refined, concentrated and elevated above ordinary prosaic concerns, mirroring the intensity of their emotions.

This book, *Remembered Kisses*, is a celebration of love which draws upon a selection of Irish poetry and paintings. Each poem is accompanied by a picture, chosen not in order to illustrate it but to complement it. Indeed, you could transpose the elements of that last sentence, placing the paintings first. For those elements are so sensitively blended in this selection as to leave one puzzling over which came first in any instance, poem or picture.

Take, for example, Yeats' 'He Wishes for the Cloths of Heaven', one of a series of poems which comprises much of his third published volume, *The Wind Among the Reeds* (1899). All were inspired by his unrequited love for Maud Gonne. This short poem, so *fin de siècle* in its diction and sensibility, is accompanied by Tim Goulding's 'Voyage', a semi-representational work completely modern in theme and execution. There is no direct link between poem and painting, no crude photographic coupling. They sit opposite each other on the printed page – opposite and equal, one might say – in a harmony that seems natural and uncontrived.

This book yields other pleasures beyond its formal organisation. It is no harm to have a reminder of the sheer richness of the Irish poetic tradition. Most people are familiar with W. B. Yeats' position in the pantheon of English-language poets. But long before Yeats, there was an ancient and vigorous tradition of verse-making in Ireland, both in Irish and in English. Yeats' achievement, massive though it is, is part of a self-renewing tradition. One thinks of great names like Swift and Goldsmith, but also of poets as varied as Thomas Moore and Sir Samuel Ferguson. It is particularly pleasing to see the work of Francis Ledwidge here. The son of an evicted tenant in Co. Meath, he had little formal education and worked as a farm labourer, yet he had a lyric gift that many an educated person might have envied. Tragically, he was killed on the Western Front in the Great War three weeks short of his thirtieth birthday.

It was often said, in the forties and fifties, that Irish poets were oppressed by the giant shadow of Yeats. If so, it has proved to be a fruitful oppression. Twentieth-century Ireland has been a powerhouse of fine poets – indeed, of fine writers in general. I write this only a few days after Seamus Heaney collected the Nobel Prize for Literature in Stockholm. A few weeks earlier, there were long queues in a Dublin bookshop as Derek Mahon signed copies of his latest volume. Both poets are present in this selection, along with a representative number of their contemporaries.

Mention of Heaney and Mahon reminds us of the extraordinary contribution of Ulster poets in the modern Irish tradition. Northern Ireland, with its division of national allegiances, is heavy with a tension that conduces to good writing. Irony, ambiguity, uncertainty: the very tools of the poet's trade lie all around in Ulster life. The title of this volume, indeed, is taken from a long poem by the best Ulster poet of an earlier generation, Louis MacNeice.

No less remarkable at the present time is the emergence of a whole school of Irish women poets. Their work is present in *Remembered Kisses* in the persons of

A Cottage Garden at Sunset
DAVID WOODLOCK 1842-1929

Paula Meehan and Eavan Boland, among others. Literature in general has been cheated by the relative silence of women. The Irish case has been worse than most, reflecting the puritanism of what used to be called traditional Ireland but which is really nothing more than post-Famine Ireland. Nowhere was the silence of women more lamentable than in the area of love poetry. That silence is now well and truly broken: in these pages you will find Rita Ann Higgins' 'It's Platonic' cohabiting with Eric Dodds' 'When the Ecstatic Body Grips' – just to take the examples of two highly charged poems of erotic sensibility. A sense of erotic rapture was not always the most distinguishing characteristic of Irish poetry in the past and the sequestered corners which it did inhabit were definitely male, a sort of poetic locker room. No longer, thank goodness: Irish women now write with an unself-conscious frankness which enriches us all.

Yet, while it is good to be reminded of the continuing vigour of Irish poetry, there is an equal joy to be had from the paintings reproduced in this book. Indeed, the quality of some of this work is startling, for a reason which is easily explained. There is no consciousness in the public mind of a developed or established Irish tradition in the visual arts. We are, according to our own propaganda, people of the word not the eye. Open this book and think again.

We know about Jack Yeats. His international reputation as a twentieth-century painter of the first rank is secure. But what of other Irish artists, of this century and others, whose works are here?

There is a body of craftsmanly excellence in these pages that delights the eye. Some of Lavery's work, for example, is particularly noteworthy in his sheer technical mastery, although heightened in his case by the emotional charge he brought to the paintings in which his wife, Hazel, served as his model. 'The Red Hammock' is a telling example, combining an academician's painterly skill with an eye for the lusciousness of colour derived in part from the Impressionists. The result has an air of almost oriental luxury about it.

Yeats *père et fils* are also here, making it a treble for that remarkable family. John Butler Yeats' 'Portrait of Sarah Alice Lawson' is indicative of his deserved reputation in this genre. As for Jack, take your pick. Has any painter anywhere ever used colour more exuberantly than he? There is a sheer Barnum & Bailey assertiveness about Jack Yeats' painting that is irresistible.

Roderic O'Conor is an artist whose reputation, long neglected, is now enjoying a deserved revival. His versatility of technique is well demonstrated in the contrasting brushwork between 'Seated Nude' and 'Girl in a Green Sweater', a

A Garden in France
SIR JOHN LAVERY 1856-1941

portrait charged with atmosphere and ambiguity. There is nothing merely decorative or commemorative here, rather the psychological penetration that distinguishes good portraiture in any medium.

Another outstanding portraitist whose reputation, although considerable in his day, is now reviving following his fall from fashionable grace, is Sir William Orpen. The lusciousness of his women is very marked. Although restrained by the demands of academic propriety, the erotic signals in some of his paintings are unmistakeable. His marvellously suggestive 'Nude Study, 1906' is a superb example.

In the end, it is the conjunction of verse and paint that makes this book worthwhile. It is impossible to analyse or introduce the two elements as an organic unity, yet the failure to do so sells the book short. For it is exactly that mysterious unity, in which the elements are subsumed into each other while remaining independent, that makes it work. In this, it is like a perfect love affair. It is a union of equals, which does not destroy or oppress the separate personalities, but launches them – together – into a higher orbit.

Louis Bell, Dublin, 1996

L'Amitié

She allows me to kiss her twice, as though to say,
'Yes, my entire goodwill is yours, my friend.
We understand each other: or, at least,
We strive to make our mutual mystery end.'

But nothing ends that mystery. My thoughts
Go back to when — comparative strangers — we
Discussed a dozen earnest trifles, yet
Endowed them with a strange intensity;

And how weeks later, once, I saw you come
Into a room, dressed for some grand affair
In silk, and for ten minutes could admire
The straight division in your well-brushed hair,

And feel, 'She's lovely, very lovely. Men
Have turned less loveliness than this to rhyme.'
Yet, never, in the craziest flight of hope,
Imagined, then, that there could come a time

When we would kiss as friends. But now I see
Kisses, or even love itself, must be
Almost, and to the very end, mere balm
Given to assuage that mutual mystery.

Children stand tiptoe at a fence of wood,
And all they glimpse seems as by magic made:
So, in the lovely tumult of our days,
The heart stands tiptoe at its palisade.

MONK GIBBON 1896-1987

Portrait of Miss Jennie Simson
SIR WILLIAM ORPEN 1878-1931

Caravan in Sunlight
FRANK MCKELVEY 1895-1974

Sunup

The sun kisses my eyes open:
Another day of wanting you.
I'd like to kiss your eyes again,
No comfort now in being alone.

Is she delighting you in bed
In her caravan on a cutaway road?
Does the sun give you the same kiss
To wake you, with her at your side?

I kiss you both, like the sun,
I kiss your hands and your feet,
Your ears and your eyes,
Both your bodies, I bless them both.

Do you feel this when you make love?
Do you love her as I loved you!
Will you let her steal all you have
And suffer her to leave?

Meet me today! We'll find a wood
Of blackthorn in white bud:
And let me give you one more kiss
Full of sun, free of bitterness.

RICHARD MURPHY 1927-

Song

When thy Beauty appears
In its Graces and Airs,
   All bright as an Angel new dropt from the Sky;
At distance I gaze, and am aw'd by my Fears,
   So strangely you dazzle my Eye!

But when without Art,
Your kind Thoughts you impart,
   When your Love runs in Blushes thro' ev'ry Vein;
When it darts from your Eyes, when it pants in your Heart,
   Then I know you're a Woman again.

There's a Passion and Pride
In our Sex, (she reply'd,)
   And thus (might I gratify both) I wou'd do:
Still an Angel appeart to each Lover beside,
   But still be a Woman to you.

THOMAS PARNELL 1679-1718

Hazel, Lady Lavery at an Easel
SIR JOHN LAVERY 1856-1941

Portrait of Mary Potter
SIR ROBERT PONSONBY STAPLES 1853-1943

Do You?

You came for Sunday afternoon,
You stayed for tea
And look what you left behind —
Every memory, sheafed carelessly on my window seat,
Of you and someone who looks sadly,
Sadly, sadly like me.
I sometimes think I see you
Loitering in the shrubbery
Without intent, idling nonchalantly
Under the weeping beech; I sent
Those memories, lovingly enveloped, to that
Memorable attic flat,
Someday I may even
Stand at your door,
Hopeful and
Completely uncalled for;
But distance is proving such a very thick wall
I can hardly hear you any more.
Do you feel this at all? Do you?

SARA BERKELEY 1967-

Tracks

I
The vast bedroom
a hall of air,
our linked bodies
lying there.

II
As I turn to kiss
your long, black
hair, small breasts,
heat flares from
your fragrant skin,
your eyes widen as
deeper, more certain
and often, I enter
to search possession
of where your being
hides in flesh.

III
Behind our eyelids
a landscape opens,

a violet horizon
pilgrims labour across,
a sky of colours
that change, explode
a fantail of stars
the mental lightning
of sex illuminating
the walls of the skull;
a floating pleasure dome.

IV
I shall miss you
creaks the mirror
into which the scene
shortly disappears:
the vast bedroom
a hall of air, the
tracks of our bodies
fading there, while
giggling maids push
a trolley of fresh
linen down the corridor.

JOHN MONTAGUE 1929-

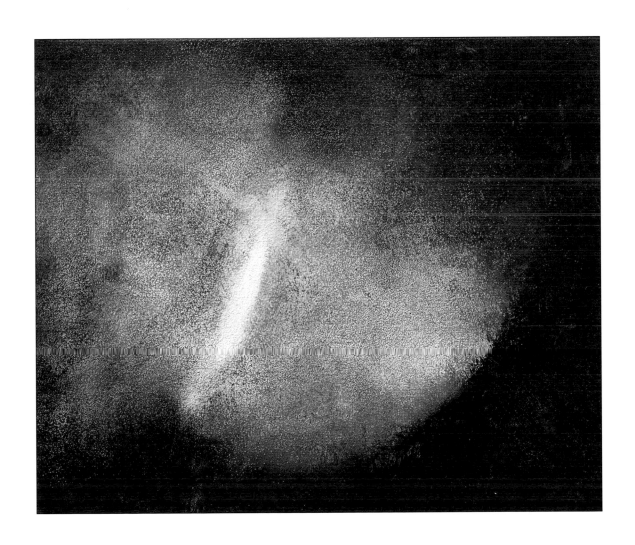

In the Realms of Light
TIM GOULDING 1945-

The Tipperary Hurler
SEAN KEATING 1889-1977

There is no deed I would not dare

There is no deed I would not dare
   Unloving, but to gain your smile,
No shame or sorrow I would not share
   (Though withering in a wintery while)
If I could win your friendship's grace
   While Time's slow pace is lagging still
Though my lost heart should leave no trace
   Of Love on Heaven's immortal will.

There is no death I would not crave
   If thus I'd save your heart from tears;
To snatch your glory from the grave
   I'd brave all fates and feel no fears
Although my heart be calm and cold
   And feel no flame nor mirth of Love
Nor buoyed with hope be overbold
   To seize and hold the Shining Dove.

But I do love you and I know
   Nor any deed nor difficult quest
To try to compass, that would show
   The fire that burns within my breast;
I cannot draw the dazzling blade
   My body sheathes, Love's splendid sword,
Lest you be blinded — and dismayed
   To silence fall my wounded word.

If I would do each desperate thing
   Only to bring you ease or mirth
What pinnacle for Love's strong wing
   Towers above the heights of Earth?
I cannot give your soul belief
   In the great visions of my heart,
I cannot, and it is my grief
   Do aught to please — but depart.

JOSEPH MARY PLUNKETT 1887-1916

Lines of Leaving

I am losing you again
all again
as if you were ever mine to lose.
The pain is as deep
beyond formal possession
beyond the fierce frivolity of tears.

Absurdly you came into my world
my time-wrecked world
a quiet laugh below the thunder.
Absurdly you leave it now
as always I foreknew you would.
I lived on an alien joy.

Your gentleness disarmed me
wine in my desert
peace across impassable seas
path of light in my jungle.

Now uncatchable as the wind you go
beyond the wind
and there is nothing in my world
save the straw of salvation in the amber dream.
The absurdity of that vast improbable joy.
The absurdity of you gone.

CHRISTY BROWN 1932-1981

Female Nude Study
ANONYMOUS, IRISH SCHOOL, 20TH CENTURY

Molly Macree
THOMAS JONES 1823-1893

Dear Black Head

Put your head, darling, darling, darling,
Your darling black head my heart above;
Oh, mouth of honey, with the thyme for fragrance,
Who, with heart in breast, could deny you love?
Oh, many and many a young girl for me is pining,
Letting her locks of gold to the cold wind free,
For me, the foremost of our gay young fellows;
But I'd leave a hundred, pure love, for thee!
Then put your head, darling, darling, darling,
Your darling black head my heart above;
Oh, mouth of honey, with the thyme for fragrance,
Who, with heart in breast, could deny you love?

From the Irish
SIR SAMUEL FERGUSON *1810-1886*

Letters from the island

The scrubland moistens round your feet at every spongy step,
And there's a cave under the south cliff
That thuds like a dull cannon to the lashes of the sea.
Over the slope, a baldy pebbled beach dragged by slimy seaweed.
You feel that if you cupped your hands to lift
The water, it would look a drowned grey-green.

A spring spurts peatish on the hill.
We've stood there, bare in the rain,
And laughed and sang the seagulls hoarse.
And then we'd wander off apart —
Happy when we sought each other out.

And when we slept the day
And crouched, reading in the night,
Keeping lit the flur of turf, and brewing tea,
The paraffin-mellow glimmer burning at our eyes.

Just once there was a calmness in the sky,
When the ridge of pines stopped fighting.
And he talked his heart onto the moon.
There was no closeness that was close enough.
We tried to grind our bones into the rock —
To drown the gash of water throbbing in the cave
By our own hot gasps.

All night the wind and rain
Whee'd and oo'd around our shack.
He lit the lamp.
And I, in our warm cove of blankets,
Watched his naked shadow darkening the rafters.
Early in the weak washed light I try
To think the thoughts that move his sleeping face.

But the boat will come tomorrow.

JOAN NEWMANN 1942-

Summer Evening, Achill
MICHEAL J. DE BURCA 1913-1985

She is far from the land

She is far from the land where her young hero sleeps
   And lovers are round her, sighing;
But coldly she turns from their gaze, and weeps,
   For her heart in his grave is lying.

She sings the wild song of her dear native plains,
   Every note which he lov'd awaking; —
Ah! little they think who delight in her strains,
   How the heart of the Minstrel is breaking.

He had liv'd for his love, for his country he died,
   They were all that to life had entwin'd him;
Nor soon shall the tears of his country be dried,
   Nor long will his love stay behind him.

Oh! make her a grave where the sunbeams rest,
   When they promise a glorious morrow;
They'll shine o'er her sleep, like a smile from the West,
   From her own lov'd island of sorrow.

THOMAS MOORE 1779-1852

Resting
SIR WILLIAM ORPEN 1878-1931

The Falconer
DANIEL MACLISE *1806-1870*

'Tis All for Thee

If life for me hath joy or light.
   'Tis all from thee,
My thoughts by day, my dreams by night,
   Are but of thee, of only thee.
Whate'er of hope or peace I know,
My zest in joy, my balm in woe,
To those dear eyes of thine I owe,
   'Tis all from thee.

My heart, ev'n ere I saw those eyes,
   Seem'd doom'd to thee;
Kept pure till then from other ties,
   'Twas all for thee, for only thee.
Like plants that sleep, till sunny May
Calls forth their life, my spirit lay,
Till, touch'd by Love's awak'ning ray,
   It liv'd for thee, it liv'd for thee.

When Fame would call me to her heights,
   She speaks by thee;
And dim would shine her proudest lights,
   Unshar'd by thee, unshar'd by thee.
Whene'er I seek the Muse's shrine,
Where Bards have hung their wreaths divine,
And wish those wreaths of glory mine,
   'Tis all for thee, for only thee.

THOMAS MOORE 1779-1852

My Grief on the Sea

My grief on the sea
How the waves of it roll!
For they heave between me
And the love of my soul!

Abandoned, forsaken,
To grief and to care,
Will the sea ever waken
Relief from despair?

My grief, and my trouble!
Would he and I were
In the province of Leinster,
Or the county of Clare.

Were I and my darling —
Oh, heart-bitter wound! —
On board of the ship
For America bound.

On a green bed of rushes
All last night I lay,
And I flung it abroad
With the heat of the day.

And my love came behind me —
He came from the south;
His breast to my bosom,
His mouth to my mouth.

From the Irish
DOUGLAS HYDE *1860-1949*

Gathering Kelp
WILLIAM MAGRATH 1838-1918

With Flowers

These have more language than my song,
  Take them and let them speak for me.
I whispered them a secret thing
  Down in the green lanes of Allary.

You shall remember quiet ways
  Watching them fade, and quiet eyes
And two hearts given up to love,
  A foolish and an overwise.

FRANCIS LEDWIDGE 1887-1917

Sunlight on the Floor
PATRICK HENNESSY *1915-1980*

Autumn Journal

from Canto IV

September has come, it is *hers*
    Whose vitality leaps in the autumn,
Whose nature prefers
    Trees without leaves and a fire in the fireplace;
So I give her this month and the next
    Though the whole of my year should be hers who has rendered already
So many of its days intolerable or perplexed
    But so many more so happy;
Who has left a scent on my life and left my walls
    Dancing over and over with her shadow,
Whose hair is twined in all my waterfalls
    And all of London littered with remembered kisses.
So I am glad
    That life contains her with her moods and moments
More shifting and more transient than I had
    Yet thought of as being integral to beauty;
Whose mind is like the wind on a sea of wheat,
    Whose eyes are candour,
And assurance in her feet
    Like a homing pigeon never by doubt diverted.
To whom I send my thanks
    That the air has become shot silk, the streets are music,
And that the ranks
    Of men are ranks of men, no more of ciphers.

So that if now alone
    I must pursue this life, it will not be only
A drag from numbered stone to numbered stone
    But a ladder of angels, river turning tidal.
Off-hand, at times hysterical, abrupt,
    You are one I always shall remember,
Whom cant can never corrupt
    Nor argument disinherit.
Frivolous, always in a hurry, forgetting the address,
    Frowning too often, taking enormous notice
Of hats and backchat — how could I assess
    The thing that makes you different?
You whom I remember glad or tired,
    Smiling in drink or scintillating anger,
Inopportunely desired
    On boats, on trains, on roads when walking.
Sometimes untidy, often elegant,
    So easily hurt, so readily responsive,
To whom a trifle could be an irritant
    Or could be balm and manna.
Whose words would tumble over each other and pelt
    From pure excitement,
Whose fingers curl and melt
    When you were friendly.
I shall remember you in bed with bright
    Eyes or in a café stirring coffee
Abstractedly and on your plate the white
    Smoking stub your lips had touched with crimson.
And I shall remember how your words could hurt

Because they were so honest
And even your lies were able to assert
  Integrity of purpose.
And it is on the strength of knowing you
  I reckon generous feeling more important
Than the mere deliberating what to do
  When neither the pros nor cons affect the pulses.
And though I have suffered from your special strength
  Who never flatter for points nor fake responses
I should be proud if I could evolve at length
  An equal thrust and pattern.

LOUIS MACNEICE 1907-1963

September Gale
JACK B. YEATS 1871-1957

Portrait of Kitsy Franklin
GEORGE RUSSELL (AE) 1867-1935

Girl of the Red Mouth

Girl of the red mouth,
  Love me! Love me!
Girl of the red mouth,
   Love me!
'Tis by its curve, I know,
Love fashioneth his bow,
And bends it — ah, even so!
  Oh, girl of the red mouth, love me!

Girl of the blue eye,
  Love me! Love me!
Girl of the dew eye,
   Love me!
Worlds hang for lamps on high;
And thought's world lives in thy
Lustrous and tender eye —
  Oh, girl of the blue eye, love me!

Girl of the swan's neck,
  Love me! Love me!
Girl of the swan's neck,
   Love me!
As marble Greek doth grow
To his steed's back of snow,
Thy white neck sits thy shoulder so —
  Oh, girl of the swan's neck, love me!

Girl of the low voice,
  Love me! Love me!
Girl of the sweet voice,
   Love me!
Like the echo of a bell —
Like the bubbling of a well —
Sweeter! Love within doth dwell —
  Oh, girl of the low voice, love me!

MARTIN MACDERMOTT 1823-1905

A Bend in the River Lee
CECIL GALBALLY 1911-1995

The Alteration

I knew all solitude, it seemed
  That any man might know
Dead year met year, and then I dreamed
  I might have comfort so.

But now when you and I apart
  Must pass two days or three
Then in the desert of my heart
  I perish utterly.

JOHN MILLINGTON SYNGE 1871-1909

The Tinsel Scarf
WILLIAM LEECH *1881-1968*

Oh, call it by some better name

Oh, call it by some better name,
  For Friendship sounds too cold,
While Love is now a worldly flame,
  Whose shrine must be of gold;
And Passion, like the sun at noon,
  That burns o'er all he sees,
Awhile as warm, will set as soon —
  Then, call it none of these.

Imagine something purer far,
  More free from stain of clay
Than Friendship, Love, or Passion are,
  Yet human still as they:
And if thy lip, for love like this,
  No mortal word can frame,
Go, ask of angels what it is,
  And call it by that name!

THOMAS MOORE 1779-1852

To You

In the old days of bitter faces
And cold eyes
I would go to the lone, large places, the hills
And the skies,
To the twilight of grey, great shadows
And bird cries ...
And shadows would hide me, and wind sighed
With my sighs
But you, my Jewess, having come, and gone,
Whence can I bring my soul
When the winds but mock, and the shadows
Bring mirrors of thy soul?

CHARLES DONNELLY 1914-1937

Man in Red with his Horse
HUGH HAMILTON 1740-1808

Grace by Candlelight
SIR WILLIAM ORPEN *1878-1931*

Do You Remember That Night?

Do you remember that night
When you were at the window
With neither hat nor gloves
Nor coat to shelter you?
I reached out my hand to you
And you ardently grasped it,
I remained to converse with you
Until the larks began to sing.

Do you remember that night
That you and I were
At the foot of the rowan-tree
And the night drifting snow?
Your head on my breast,
And your pipe sweetly playing?
Little thought I that night
That our love ties would loosen!

Beloved of my inmost heart,
Come some night, and soon,
When my people are at rest,
That we may talk together.
My arms shall encircle you
While I relate my sad tale,
That your soft, pleasant converse
Hath deprived me of heaven.

The fire is unraked,
The light unextinguished,
The key under the door,
Do you softly draw it.
My mother is asleep,
But I am wide awake;
My fortune in my hand,
I am ready to go with you.

From the Irish
EUGENE O'CURRY *1796-1862*

Voyage
TIM GOULDING 1945-

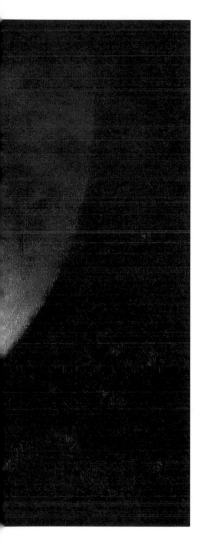

He Wishes for the Cloths of Heaven

Had I the heavens' embroidered cloths,
Enwrought with golden and silver light,
The blue and the dim and the dark cloths
Of night and light and the half-light,
I would spread the cloths under your feet:
But I, being poor, have only my dreams;
I have spread my dreams under your feet;
Tread softly because you tread on my dreams.

WILLIAM BUTLER YEATS 1865-1939

The Refugee
SIR WILLIAM ORPEN 1878-1931

Amores I,V

The day being humid and my head
heavy, I stretched out on a bed.
The open window to the right
reflected woodland-watery light,
a keyed-up silence as of dawn
or dusk, the vibrant and uncertain
hour when a brave girl might undress
and caper naked on the grass.
You entered in a muslin gown,
bare-footed, your fine braids undone,
a fabled goddess with an air
as if in heat yet debonair.
Aroused, I grabbed and roughly tore
until your gown squirmed on the floor.
Oh, you resisted, but like one
who knows resistance is in vain;
and, when you stood revealed, my eyes
feasted on shoulders, breasts and thighs.
I held you hard and down you slid
beside me, as we knew you would.
Oh, come to me again as then you did!

From Ovid in Love
DEREK MAHON 1941-

Ready for Flight

From this I will not swerve nor fall nor falter:
If around your heart the crowds disperse,
And I who at their whim now freeze or swelter
Am allowed to come to a more temperate place,

And if a runner starts to run to me
Dispatched by you, crying that all is trampled
Underfoot, terraces smashed, the entry
Into holy places rudely sampled,

Then I would come at once my love with love
Bringing to wasted areas the sight
Of butterfly and swan and turtle dove
Their wings ruffled like sails ready for flight.

In such surroundings, after the decease
Of devils, you and I would live in peace.

EAVAN BOLAND 1945-

Harbour, Bangor
COLIN MIDDLETON 1910-1983

When You are Old

When you are old and grey and full of sleep,
And nodding by the fire, take down this book,
And slowly read, and dream of the soft look
Your eyes had once, and of their shadows deep;

How many loved your moments of glad grace,
And loved your beauty with love false or true,
But one man loved the pilgrim soul in you,
And loved the sorrows of your changing face;

And bending down beside the glowing bars,
Murmur, a little sadly, how Love fled
And paced upon the mountains overhead
And hid his face amid a crowd of stars.

WILLIAM BUTLER YEATS 1865-1939

Portrait of the Artist's Mother, Mrs H.E. Clarke
CAREY CLARKE PRHA 1936-

An Samhradh Samh
MURIEL BRANDT 1909-1981

At Ards

All day the pheasants were honking
like vintage cars and
the cows cropped
young grass with a sound of
rending cloth. The ferns
were uncurling their croziers under
the candelabra of the chestnuts and
the hills were blue, blue as
the pools of bluebells in the grass. There was
a smell of crushed
almonds in the airs eddying
from the whins and
you were there with
a flower in your hand and I
was with you and I wanted
to take your other hand but
the children were there
as well and the cows.
I knew they would stare.

FRANCIS HARVEY 1925-

King O'Toole
SEAN KEATING 1889-1977

Cashel of Munster

I'd wed you without herds, without money, or rich array,
And I'd wed you on a dewy morn at day-dawn grey;
My bitter woe it is, love, that we are not far away
In Cashel town, though the bare deal board were our marriage-bed this day!

Oh, fair maid, remember the green hill side,
Remember how I hunted about the valleys wide;
Time now has worn me; my locks are turn'd to grey,
The year is scarce and I am poor, but send me not, love, away!

Oh, deem not my blood is of base strain, my girl;
Oh, deem not my birth was as the birth of the churl;
Marry me, and prove me, and say soon you will,
That noble blood is written on my right side still!

My purse holds no red gold, no coin of the silver white,
No herds are mine to drive through the long twilight!
But the pretty girl that would take me, all bare though I be and lone,
Oh, I'd take her with me kindly to the county Tyrone.

Oh, my girl, I can see 'tis in trouble you are,
And, oh, my girl, I see 'tis your people's reproach you bear:
— *I am a girl in trouble for his sake with whom I fly,*
And, oh, may no other maiden know such reproach as I!

From the Irish
SIR SAMUEL FERGUSON *1810-1886*

Love Song

Sweet in her green dell the Flower of Beauty slumbers
    Lulled by the faint breezes sighing through her hair;
Sleeps she and hears not the melancholy numbers
    Breathed to my sad lute 'mid the lonely air.

Down from the high cliffs the rivulet is teeming
    To wind round the willow banks that lure him from above;
O that in tears, from my rocky prison streaming,
    I too could glide to the bower of my love!

Ah where the woodbines with sleepy arms have wound her,
    Opes she her eyelids at the dream of my lay,
Listening, like the dove, while the fountains echo round her,
    To her lost mate's call in the forests far away.

Come, then, my bird! For the peace thou ever bearest,
    Still heaven's messenger of comfort to me,
Come, this fond bosom, O faithfulest and fairest,
    Bleeds with its death-wound its wound of love for thee.

GEORGE DARLEY 1795-1846

Portrait of Annie Callwell
SIR FREDERICK BURTON *1816-1900*

Words

Were I this forest pool
And you the birch tree bending over,
Your thoughts in shaken leaves could drop
Upon my heart. And we would never
So fret our happiness taming
Rebellious words that sulk, run crazy
And gibber like caged monkeys,
Mocking their tamers.

C. DAY LEWIS 1904-1972

Strickland's Glen, Bangor
SAMUEL MCCLOY 1831-1904

Les Sylphides

Life in a day: he took his girl to the ballet;
Being shortsighted himself could hardly see it —
    The white skirts in the grey
      Glade and the swell of the music
      Lifting the white sails.

Calyx upon calyx, canterbury bells in the breeze
The flowers on the left mirror to the flowers on the right
    And the naked arms above
      The powdered faces moving
      Like seaweed in a pool.

Now, he thought, we are floating — ageless, oarless —
Now there is no separation, from now on
    You will be wearing white
      Satin and a red sash
      Under the waltzing trees.

But the music stopped, the dancers took their curtain,
The river had come to a lock — a shuffle of programmes —
    And we cannot continue down
      Stream unless we are ready
      To enter the lock and drop.

So they were married — to be the more together —
And found they were never again so much together,
 Divided by the morning tea,
 By the evening paper,
 By children and tradesmen's bills.

Waking at times in the night she found assurance
Due to his regular breathing but wondered whether
 It was really worth it and where
 The river had flowed away
 And where were the white flowers.

from Novelettes
LOUIS MACNEICE 1907-1963

Memory of 'Les Sylphides'
SYDNEY SMITH 1912-1982

A Song

Strephon, your breach of faith and trust
   Affords me no surprise;
A man who grateful was, or just,
   Might make my wonder rise.

That heart to you so fondly tied,
   With pleasure wore its chain,
But from your cold neglectful pride,
   Found liberty again.

For this no wrath inflames my mind,
   My thanks are due to thee;
Such thanks as generous victors find,
   Who set their captives free.

LAETITIA PILKINGTON 1712-1750

The Playboy
SEAN KEATING *1889-1977*

A Breezy Day, Howth
SIR WILLIAM ORPEN 1878-1931

Spring Love

I saw her coming through the flowery grass,
    Round her swift ankles butterfly and bee
Blent loud and silent wings; I saw her pass
    When foam-bows shivered on the sunny sea.

Then came the swallow crowding up the dawn,
    And cuckoo echoes filled the dewy South.
I left my love upon the hill, alone,
    My last kiss burning on her lovely mouth.

FRANCIS LEDWIDGE 1887-1917

While You Are Talking

While you are talking, though I seem all ears,
forgive me if you notice a stray see-through
look; on tiptoe behind the eyes' frontiers
I am spying, wondering at this mobile you.
Sometimes nurturer, praise-giver to the male,
caresser of failures, mother earth, breakwater
to my vessel, suddenly you'll appear frail —
in my arms I'll cradle you like a daughter.
Now soul pilot and I confess redemptress,
turner of new leaves, reshaper of a history;
then the spirit turns flesh — playful temptress
I untie again ribbons of your mystery.
You shift and travel as only a lover can;
one woman and all things to this one man.

MICHEAL O'SIADHAIL 1947-

Portrait of Eamon Morrissey
EDWARD MCGUIRE *1932-1986*

The Ghost

Since you that I loved are lost
   And all my hopes are vain,
Then come to me, a lonely ghost,
   Out of the night and rain.

Oh, come to me a ghost
   And sit beside my fire.
I shall not fear you, loved and lost
   And still my heart's desire.

Oh, come to me again
   When stars are bright and lean,
Oh, come and tap on the window-pane
   And I will let you in.

Eagerly will I come
   And set the window wide;
And bid you welcome to your home
   And to your own fireside.

Oh, come, belovèd ghost,
   When stars lean on the hill:
And I will warm you from the frost
   And from the night-wind chill.

You shall forget the grave,
   And I forget to weep:
Since the old comfort we shall have
   To lull us into sleep.

Fear! Is it fear of you,
   And on my breast your head?
I shall but fear the dawning new,
   And the cocks both white and red.

KATHARINE TYNAN 1861-1931

Lady in White
ESTELLA SOLOMONS *1882-1968*

Seated Nude
RODERIC O'CONOR *1860-1940*

Nessa

I met her on the First of August
In the Shangri-La Hotel,
She took me by the index finger
And dropped me in her well.
And that was a whirlpool, that was a whirlpool,
And I very nearly drowned.

Take off your pants, she said to me,
And I very nearly didn't;
Would you care to swim, she said to me,
And I hopped into the Irish sea.
And that was a whirlpool, that was a whirlpool,
And I very nearly drowned.

On the way back I fell in the field
And she fell down beside me.
I'd have lain in the grass with her all my life
With Nessa:
She was a whirlpool, she was a whirlpool,
And I very nearly drowned.

Oh Nessa my dear, Nessa my dear,
Will you stay with me on the rocks?
Will you come for me into the Irish sea
And for me let your red hair down?
And then we will ride into Dublin city
In a taxi-cab wrapped-up in dust.
Oh you are a whirlpool, you are a whirlpool,
And I am very nearly drowned.

PAUL DURCAN 1944-

'When you left the city you carried . . .'

When you left the city you carried
off the May sun, left heavy skies.
A bad spell was cast on the island:
colour leached from blossom, birds fell mute,
the Liffey stopped dreaming of the sea,
the eyes of the citizenry grew frosty
and for two weeks now I have moved
like a zombie through my life.
All I turn my hand to
snags. I can't sleep nights. I fret,
demented with desire for your body
weaving in sea motion under mine.
Close to dawn I hit the streets
and walk in hope of losing you,
in hope of peace. Christ I'd give
ten years of my span to look on your face
for an instant, to fall into your eyes
that are the sea blue of desert mornings,
to dive through the fiery coronas,
drown in the depths of your pupils.
Days are spent in superstitious rite:
penny candles at Valentine's shrine,
invocations to an Eastern goddess

to please watch over your journey,
to bring you home safe,
and if anyone should lay a finger on you
or harm a hair of your head
there'll be no hiding from my wrath
on this, or any other, planet.

PAULA MEEHAN 1955-

The Limerick Girl
SEAN KEATING 1889-1977

Prothalamium

And so must I lose her whose mind
Fitted so sweetly and securely into mine
That words seeded and blossomed in an instant,
Whose body was one of my fine
Morning visions come alive and perfect?
Must she slip out of my arms so
And I never revel again in the twilight of her hair
Or see the world grow
Marvellous within her eye? My hands
Are empty; and suddenly I think
That on some night like this, when rain is soft
And moths flutter at the window, seeking a chink,
I'll lose her utterly, a bedded bride
Gold ring and contract bound,
The night filled with terrifying music
And she not hearing a sound.

DONAGH MACDONAGH *1912-1968*

Night in a Small Town
JACK B. YEATS 1871-1957

The Otter

When you plunged
The light of Tuscany wavered
And swung through the pool
From top to bottom.

I loved your wet head and smashing crawl,
Your fine swimmer's back and shoulders
Surfacing and surfacing again
This year and every year since.

I sat dry-throated on the warm stones.
You were beyond me.
The mellowed clarities, the grape-deep air
Thinned and disappointed.

Thank God for the slow loadening,
When I hold you now
We are close and deep
As the atmosphere on water.

My two hands are plumbed water.
You are my palpable, lithe
Otter of memory
In the pool of the moment,

Turning to swim on your back,
Each silent, thigh-shaking kick
Re-tilting the light,
Heaving the cool at your neck.

And suddenly you're out,
Back again, intent as ever,
Heavy and frisky in your freshened pelt,
Printing the stones.

SEAMUS HEANEY 1939-

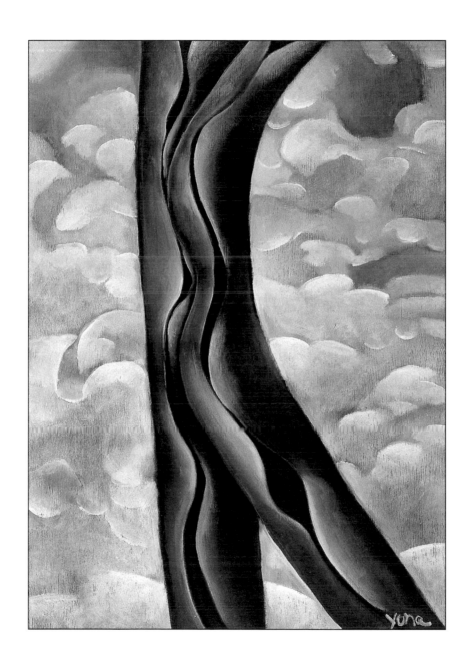

Couplet
YONA CAFFREY 1951-

In Absence

Last night I read your letters once again —
Read till the dawn filled all my room with grey;
Then quenched my light and put the leaves away,
And prayed for sleep to ease my heart's great pain.
But ah! that poignant tenderness made vain
My hope of rest — I could not sleep or pray
For thought of you, and the slow broadening day
Held me there prisoner of my throbbing brain.

Yet I did sleep before the silence broke,
And dream, but not of you — the old dreams rife
With duties which would bind me to the yoke
Of my old futile, lone, reluctant life:
I stretched my hands for help in the vain strife,
And grasped these leaves, and to this pain awoke.

THOMAS MACDONAGH 1878-1916

The Red Rose
SIR JOHN LAVERY 1856-1941

Man and a Woman
NORMAN MORROW 1879-1917

We Get Along

We get along like two
Houses on fire. We burn excitedly,
Swopping flames, crackling with joy —
Let it always be so,
O let it always.

I'm tired of going round and round,
My tail in my mouth;
Every revolution makes me fear
I've always been wrong
About everything; but we get along
Like two houses alight
And spitting stars, our laughter
Is less of a secret,
More of a shout
Into the endless, flame-shot
Night.

SARA BERKELEY 1967-

The Sorrow of Love

I saw my love in his anger
And he didn't pretend to admire,
Yet I am the vein of his heart
And the beauty of his desire.

Oh, fire in the night is my love
When anger his spirit enthralls,
Yet he is kinder to me
Than the lambs who come when I call.

He holds me with both his hands
And swears that he loves me true.
He says I am golder than gold
At the bottom of Sliav Dhu.

But he passed me coldly today
And I wish that the birds wouldn't sing,
And I wish that I was far away
At the rim of the world's ring.

FRANCIS LEDWIDGE 1887-1917

Portrait of the Artist's Sister
SIR WILLIAM ORPEN 1878-1931

They know not my heart

They know not my heart, who believe there can be
One stain of this earth in its feeling for thee;
Who think, while I see thee in beauty's young hour,
As pure as the morning's first dew on the flow'r,
I could harm what I love, — as the sun's wanton ray
But smiles on the dew-drop to waste it away.

No — beaming with light as those young features are,
There's a light round thy heart which is lovelier far:
It is not that cheek — 'tis the soul dawning clear
Thro' its innocent blush makes thy beauty so dear;
As the sky we look up to, though glorious and fair,
Is look'd up to the more, because Heaven lies there!

THOMAS MOORE 1779-1852

Lovers in a Landscape
THOMAS BRIDGEFORD *1812-1878*

Bridal Night

Weeping, murmuring, complaining,
   Lost to every gay delight;
Myra, too sincere for feigning,
   Fears th' approaching bridal night.

Yet, why impair thy bright perfection?
   Or dim thy beauty with a tear?
Had Myra followed my direction,
   She long had wanted cause of fear.

OLIVER GOLDSMITH 1728-1774

The Bridal Dress
SAMUEL MCCLOY 1831-1904

Noon at St. Michael's

Nurses and nuns —
their sails whiter than those
of the yachts in the bay, they come and go
on winged feet, most of them, or in 'sensible' shoes.
July, and I should be climbing among stones
or diving, but for broken bones,
from the rocks below.

I try to read
a new novel set aside;
but a sword-swift pain
in the left shoulder-blade, the result
of a tumble in Sheridan Square, makes reading difficult.
Writing you can do in your head.
It starts to rain

on the sea,
suddenly dark, the pier,
the gardens and the church spires of Dun Laoghaire.
You would think it was suddenly October
as smoke flaps, the yachts tack violently
and those caught in the downpour
run for cover.

But in a few
minutes the sun shines again,
the leaves and hedges glisten as if with dew
in that fragrant freshness after rain
when the world seems made anew
before confusion, before pain;
and I think of you,

a funny-face
but solemn, with the sharpest mind I know,
a thoughtful creature of unconscious grace
bent to your books in the sun or driving down
to New York for an evening on the town.
Doors open wherever you go
in that furious place;

for you are the light
rising on lost islands, the *spéir-bhean*
the old poets saw gleam in the morning mist.
When you walk down Fifth Avenue in your lavender suit,
your pony eyes opaque, I am the man
beside you, and life is bright
with the finest and best.

And I have seen,
as you have not, such is your modesty,
men turn to watch your tangle of golden hair,
your graceful carriage and unhurried air
as if you belonged to history
or '*her* story', that mystery.
You might have been

a saint or a great
courtesan, anachronistic now
in some ways, in some ways more up-to-date
than the most advanced of those we know.
While you sit on your sun-porch in Connecticut
re-reading Yeats in a feminist light,
I am there with you.

DEREK MAHON 1941-

Girl Reading, c. 1910
RODERIC O'CONOR 1860-1940

Girl with Mandolin
DANIEL O'NEILL 1920-1974

My Heart and Lute

I give thee all — I can no more —
  Though poor the off'ring be;
My heart and lute are all the store
  That I can bring to thee.
A lute whose gentle song reveals
  The soul of love full well;
And, better far, a heart that feels
  Much more than lute could tell.

Though love and song may fail, alas!
  To keep life's clouds away,
At least 'twill make them lighter pass
  Or gild them if they stay.
And ev'n if care, at moments, flings
  A discord o'er life's happy strain,
Let love but gently touch the strings,
  'Twill all be sweet again!

THOMAS MOORE 1779-1852

It's Platonic

Platonic my eye,

I yearn
for the fullness
of your tongue
making me
burst forth
pleasure after pleasure
after dark,

soaking all my dreams.

RITA ANN HIGGINS 1955-

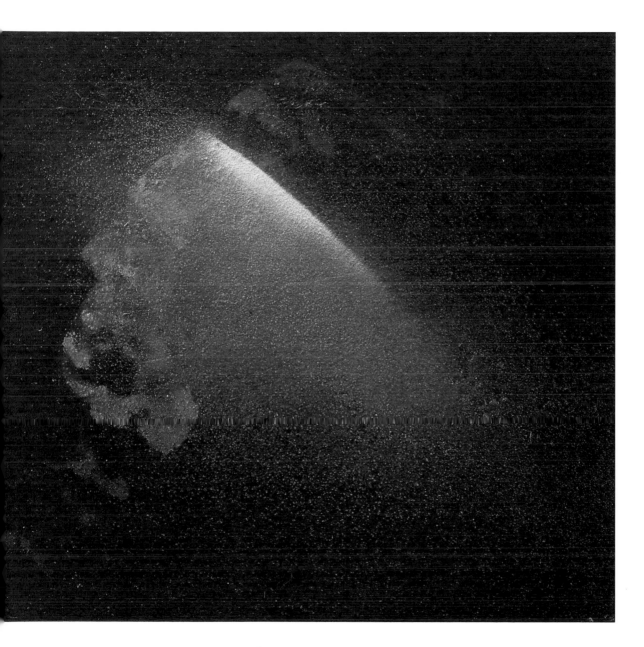

Leabharlanna Fhine Gall

Out of Darkness I
TIM GOULDING 1945-

She Moved Through the Fair

My young love said to me, 'My brothers won't mind,
And my parents won't slight you for your lack of kind.'
Then she stepped away from me, and this she did say,
'It will not be long, love, till our wedding day.'

She stepped away from me and she moved through the fair,
And fondly I watched her go here and go there,
Then she went her way homeward with one star awake,
As the swan in the evening moves over the lake.

The people were saying no two were e'er wed
But one had a sorrow that never was said,
And I smiled as she passed with her goods and her gear,
And that was the last that I saw of my dear.

I dreamt it last night that my young love came in,
So softly she entered, her feet made no din;
She came close beside me, and this she did say,
'It will not be long, love, till our wedding day.'

PÁDRAIC COLUM 1881-1972

Market Women
HUGH CHARDE 1858-1946

Portrait of John Philpott Curran
EDWARD C. GRIBBON *fl. 1931-1935*

To a Distant One

Through wild by-ways I come to you, my love,
Nor ask of those I meet the surest way,
What way I turn I cannot go astray
And miss you in my life. Though Fate may prove
A tardy guide she will not make delay
Leading me through strange seas and distant lands,
I'm coming still, though slowly, to your hands,

We'll meet one day.
There is so much to do, so little done,
In my life's space that I perforce did leave
Love at the moonlit trysting place to grieve
Till fame and other little things were won.
I have missed much that I shall not retrieve,
Far will I wander yet with much to do,
Much will I spurn before I yet meet you,

So fair I can't deceive.
Your name is in the whisper of the woods
Like Beauty calling for a poet's song
To one whose harp had suffered many a wrong
In the lean hands of Pan. And when the broods
Of flower eyes waken all the streams along
In tender whiles, I feel most near to you:—
Oh, when we meet there shall be sun and blue
Strong as the spring is strong.

FRANCIS LEDWIDGE 1887-1917

Last Night

I sat with the one I love last night
She sang to me an olden strain;
In former times it woke delight,
        Last night — but pain.

Last night we saw the stars arise,
But clouds soon dimmed the ether blue;
And when we sought each other's eyes
        Tears dimmed them too!

We paced along our favourite walk,
But paced in silence broken-hearted:
Of old we used to smile and talk;
        Last night — we parted.

GEORGE DARLEY 1795-1846

Economic Pressure
SEAN KEATING 1889-1977

Girl in a Green Sweater
RODERIC O'CONOR *1860-1940*

The Insult

It would be difficult
Even were I wise
To fault the insult
Which perfects your eyes.

Razor instincts could not cut
More deeply into mutual trust
Than this vague but yet abrupt
Penetration that goes just

To the edge of a rejection.
It is a blow that glances
Off the hard reflection
Which my self-love enhances.

Yet all that I suspect
Is arraigned in this regard.
I admire that you detect
The fears that I have frozen hard

In the ice of self-content.
Love becomes the last result
You'd expect from what you meant.
But love's my wisdom, not my fault.

SEAMUS DEANE 1940-

The Dreamers, The Geneva Window
HARRY CLARKE *1889-1931*

The Wooing of Etain

Fair lady, will you travel
To the marvellous land of stars?
Pale as snow the body there,
Under a primrose crown of hair.

No one speaks of property
In that glittering community:
White teeth shining, eyebrows black,
The foxglove hue on every cheek.

The landscape bright and speckled
As a wild bird's eggs —
However fair Ireland's Plain,
It is sad after the Great Plain!

Warm, sweet streams water the earth,
And after the choicest of wine and mead,
Those fine and flawless people
Without sin, without guilt, couple.

We can see everyone
Without being seen ourselves:
It is the cloud of Adam's transgression
Conceals us from mortal reckoning.

O woman if you join my strong clan,
Your head will hold a golden crown.
Fresh killed pork, new milk and beer,
We shall share, O Lady Fair!

From the Irish
JOHN MONTAGUE 1929-

Ice-Fields
GWEN O'DOWD *1957-*

A Postcard from Iceland

As I dipped to test the stream some yards away
From a hot spring, I could hear nothing
But the whole mud-slick muttering and boiling.

And then my guide behind me saying,
'Lukewarm. And I think you'd want to know
That *luk* was an old Icelandic word for hand.'

And you would want to know (but you know already)
How usual that waft and pressure felt
When the inner palm of water found my palm.

SEAMUS HEANEY 1939-

O Lovely Heart

O lovely heart! O Love
  No more be sorrowful
Blue are the skies above
    The Spring is beautiful
      And all the flowers
      Are blest with gentle showers.

Although the morning skies
  Are heavy now with rain
And your incredulous eyes
    Are wondering at your pain,
      Let them but weep.
      And after give them sleep.

O sorrowful! O heart
  Whose joy is difficult
Though we two are apart —
    Know you shall yet exult
      And all the years
      Be fresher for your tears.

JOSEPH MARY PLUNKETT 1887-1916

Daffodils
WALTER OSBORNE 1859-1903

The Eastern Gown
SIR WILLIAM ORPEN 1878-1931

Day and Night

I

wrapped in a sheer white negligée
   you are a fog-bound landscape
familiar but seen in a new light
   transformed by seamless mist
tantalising, trimmed with tufts of cloud
   I know that after the fog lifts
all will be sultry and warm
   I can detect a sun-like breast
already radiating through the nylon dawn

II

in hot darkness, the transistor on
   a five-note raga plays
five senses that ascend the scale of longing:
   until the gasps of music peter out
and a taut night is plucked limp
   we are out of meaning's reach
your vellum blotted with invisible ink
   my head at rest
between your breasts' parentheses

DENNIS O'DRISCOLL 1954-

I tell her she is lovely

I tell her she is lovely and she laughs,
Shy laughter altogether lovely too;
Knowing, perhaps, that it was true before;
And, when she laughs, that it is still more true.

MONK GIBBON 1896-1987

Winter, 1911
HARRIET HOCKLEY TOWNSHEND *1877-1941*

When the Ecstatic Body Grips

When the ecstatic body grips
  Its heaven, with little sobbing cries,
And lips are crushed on hot blind lips,
  I read strange pity in your eyes.

For that in you which is not mine,
  And that in you which I love best,
And that, which my day-thoughts divine
  Masterless still, still unpossessed,

Sits in the blue eyes' frightened stare,
  A naked lonely-dwelling thing,
A frail thing from its body-lair
  Drawn at my body's summoning;

Whispering low, 'O unknown man,
  Whose hunger on my hunger wrought,
Body shall give what body can,
  Shall give you all — save what you sought.'

Whispering, 'O secret one, forgive,
  Forgive and be content though still
Beyond the blood's surrender live
  The darkness of the separate will.

'Enough if in the veins we know
  Body's delirium, body's peace —
Ask not that ghost to ghost shall go,
  Essence in essence merge and cease.'

But swiftly, as in sudden sleep,
  That You in you is veiled or dead;
And the world's shrunken to a heap
  Of hot flesh huddled on a bed.

ERIC DODDS 1893-1979

Nude Study, 1906
SIR WILLIAM ORPEN 1878-1931

Wisteria
MILDRED ANN BUTLER 1858-1941

The Lover's Farewell

Slowly through the tomb-still streets I go —
　　Morn is dark, save one swart streak of gold —
Sullen rolls the far-off river's flow,
　　And the moon is very thin and cold.

Long and long before the house I stand
　　Where sleeps she, the dear, dear one I love —
All undreaming that I leave my land,
　　Mute and mourning, like the moon above!

Wishfully I stretch abroad mine arms
　　Towards the well-remembered casement-cell —
Fare thee well! Farewell thy virgin charms!
　　And thou stilly, stilly house, farewell!

And farewell the dear dusk little room,
　　Redolent of roses as a dell,
And the lattice that relieved its gloom —
　　And its pictured lilac walls, farewell!

Forth upon my path! I must not wait —
　　Bitter blows the fretful morning wind:
Warden, wilt thou softly close the gate
　　When thou knowest I leave my heart behind?

JAMES CLARENCE MANGAN 1803-1849

A South American Ode

In all my Enna's beauties blest,
   Amidst profusion still I pine;
For though she gives me up her breast,
   Its panting tenant is not mine.

OLIVER GOLDSMITH 1728-1774

The Unfinished Harmony
SIR JOHN LAVERY *1856-1941*

I want to talk to thee

I want to talk to thee of many things
Or sit in silence when the robin sings
His little song, when comes the winter bleak
I want to sit beside thee, cheek to cheek.

I want to hear thy voice my name repeat,
To fill my heart with echoes ever sweet;
I want to hear thy love come calling me
I want to seek and find but thee, but thee.

I want to talk to thee of little things
So fond, so frail, so foolish that one clings
To keep them ours — who could but understand
A joy in speaking them, thus hand in hand

Beside the fire; our joys, our hopes, our fears,
Our secret laughter, or unchidden tears;
Each day old dreams come back with beating wings,
I want to speak of these forgotten things.

I want to feel thy arms around me pressed,
To hide my weeping eyes upon thy breast;
I want thy strength to hold and comfort me
For all the grief I had in losing thee.

DORA SIGERSON 1866-1918

Portrait of the Artist's Wife
SIR WILLIAM ORPEN 1878-1931

The Death of Ailill

When there was heard no more the war's loud sound,
And only the rough corn-crake filled the hours,
And hill winds in the furze and drowsy flowers,
Maeve in her chamber with her white head bowed
On Ailill's heart was sobbing: 'I have found
The way to love you now,' she said, and he
Winked an old tear away and said: 'The proud
Unyielding heart loves never.' And then she:
'I love you now, tho' once when we were young
We walked apart like two who were estranged
Because I loved you not, now all is changed.'
And he who loved her always called her name
And said: 'You do not love me; 'tis your tongue
Talks in the dusk; you love the blazing gold
Won in the battles, and the soldier's fame.
You love the stories that are often told
By poets in the hall.' Then Maeve arose
And sought her daughter Findebar: 'Oh, child,
Go tell your father that my love went wild
With all my wars in youth, and say that now
I love him stronger than I hate my foes …'
And Findebar unto her father sped
And touched him gently on the rugged brow,
And knew by the cold touch that he was dead.

FRANCIS LEDWIDGE 1887-1917

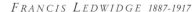

The Death of Adonis
JAMES BARRY 1741-1806

Self-portrait
JOHN LUKE 1906-1975

Between

As we fall into step I ask a penny for your thoughts.
'Oh, nothing,' you say, 'well, nothing so easily bought.'

Sliding into the rhythm of your silence, I almost forget
how lonely I'd been until that autumn morning we met.

At bedtime up along my childhood's stairway, tongues
of fire cast shadows. Too earnest, too highstrung.

My desire is endless: others ended when I'd only started.
Then, there was you: so whole-hog, so wholehearted.

Think of the thousands of nights and the shadows fought.
And the mornings of light. I try to read your thought.

In the strange openness of your face, I'm powerless.
Always this love. Always this infinity between us.

MICHEAL O'SIADHAIL 1947-

Come, rest in this bosom

Come, rest in this bosom, my own stricken deer!
Though the herd have fled from thee, thy home is still here;
Here still is the smile that no cloud can o'ercast,
And the heart and the hand all thy own to the last!

Oh! what was love made for, if 'tis not the same
Through joy and through torments, through glory and shame?
I know not, I ask not, if guilt's in that heart,
I but know that I love thee, whatever thou art!

Thou hast call'd me thy Angel in moments of bliss,
Still thy angel I'll be, 'mid the horrors of this —
Through the furnace, unshrinking, thy steps to pursue,
And shield thee, and save thee, or perish there too!

THOMAS MOORE 1779-1852

Leabharlanna Fhine Gall

The Red Hammock
SIR JOHN LAVERY 1856-1941

Index of Poets and Poems

Index of Artists and Paintings

Index of First Lines

Portrait of Sarah Alice Lawson
JOHN B. YEATS 1839-1922

Acknowledgements

Grateful acknowledgement is made to the following for permission to reprint the poems and the paintings in this book. All possible care has been made to trace ownership of selections and to make full acknowledgement. If any errors or omissions have occurred, they will be corrected in subsequent editions, provided that notification is sent to the publisher.

POETRY

SARA BERKELEY: 'Do You', reprinted by permission of Bloodaxe Books Ltd from *Facts about Water*, Bloodaxe Books, 1994, and 'We Get Along', reprinted by permission of Raven Arts Press from *Home Movie Nights* published by Raven Arts Press/Thistledown Press, 1989.

EAVAN BOLAND: 'Ready for Flight', reprinted by permission of Carcanet Press Ltd from *Collected Poems*, 1995.

CHRISTY BROWN: 'Lines of Leaving', reprinted by permission of Reed Consumer Books from *Collected Poems* published by Secker & Warburg, 1982.

PÁDRAIC COLUM: 'She Moved Through the Fair', reprinted by permission of The Estate of Pádraic Colum from *The Poet's Circuits*, published by Oxford University Press, 1960.

C. DAY LEWIS: 'Words', reprinted from *The Complete Poems of C. Day Lewis*, Sinclair Stevenson, 1992 copyright © The Estate of C. Day Lewis.

SEAMUS DEANE: 'The Insult', reprinted by permission of the author and The Gallery Press, Loughcrew, Oldcastle, Co. Meath, Ireland, from *Selected Poems*, 1988.

ERIC R. DODDS: 'When the Ecstatic Body Grips', reprinted from *Thirty-five Poems* by permission of Constable Publishers and Mr D. Russell.

CHARLES DONNELLY: 'To You', reprinted by permission of Mr J. Donnelly.

PAUL DURCAN: 'Nessa', reprinted by permission of the author from *The Selected Paul Durcan*, published by Blackstaff Press, 1983.

MONK GIBBON: 'I tell her she is lovely' and 'L'Amitié', reprinted by permission of Ms P. Cabot from *The Velvet Bow and Other Poems*, published by Martin Secker & Warburg, 1972.

FRANCIS HARVEY: 'At Ards', reprinted by permission of the author and The Gallery Press, Loughcrew, Oldcastle, Co. Meath, Ireland, from *In the Light on the Stones*, 1978.

SEAMUS HEANEY: 'The Otter' and 'A Postcard from Iceland', reprinted by permission of the author and Faber and Faber Ltd, London, and Farrar, Straus and Giroux, Inc, New York, from *Field Work* © 1976, 1979 by Seamus Heaney and *The Haw Lantern* © 1987 by Seamus Heaney.

RITA ANN HIGGINS: 'It's Platonic', reprinted by permission of Poolbeg Group Services Ltd from *Philomena's Revenge*, published by Salmon Publishing Ltd, 1992.

DOUGLAS HYDE: 'My Grief on the Sea', reprinted by permission of Mr D. Sealy.

DONAGH MacDONAGH: 'Prothalamium', reprinted by permission of Faber and Faber Ltd, London, from *The Hungry Grass*, 1947.

LOUIS MacNEICE: Extract from Canto IV, 'Autumn Journal' and 'Les Sylphides' from 'Novelettes', reprinted by permission of David Higham Associates, London, from *The Collected Poems of Louis MacNeice*, published by Faber and Faber, 1966.

DEREK MAHON: 'Noon at St. Michael's' © Derek Mahon reprinted by permission of the author from *The Hudson Letter*, 1995, published by The Gallery Press, Loughcrew, Oldcastle, Co. Meath, Ireland, and 'Amores I,V' from *Ovid in Love* © Derek Mahon reprinted by permission of the author from *Derek Mahon: Selected Poems*, published by Viking/Gallery 1991.

PAULA MEEHAN: 'When you left the city you carried…', reprinted by permission of the author and The Gallery Press, Loughcrew, Oldcastle, Co. Meath, Ireland, from *Pillow Talk*, 1994.

JOHN MONTAGUE: 'Tracks' and 'The Wooing of Etain', reprinted by permission of the author and The Gallery Press, Loughcrew, Oldcastle, Co. Meath, Ireland, from *New Selected Poems*, 1989.

RICHARD MURPHY: 'Sunup', reprinted by permission of the author from *The Price of Stone*, Faber and Faber Ltd, London, 1985.

JOAN NEWMANN: 'Letters from the island', reprinted by permission of the author and Blackstaff Press, from *Coming of Age*, 1995.

DENNIS O'DRISCOLL: 'Day and Night', reprinted by permission of the author from *Hidden Extras* by Dennis O'Driscoll, published by Anvil Press Poetry, London/Dedalus Press, Dublin, 1987.

MICHEAL O'SIADHAIL: 'Between' and 'While You Are Talking', reprinted by permission of Bloodaxe Books Ltd from *Hail! Madam Jazz* by Micheal O'Siadhail (Bloodaxe Books Ltd, 1992).

KATHARINE TYNAN: 'The Ghost', reprinted by permission of the literary executors of Pamela Hinkson.

WILLIAM BUTLER YEATS: 'He Wishes for the Cloths of Heaven' and 'When You Are Old', reprinted by permission of A.P. Watt Ltd on behalf of Michael Yeats.

PAINTINGS

AIB ART COLLECTION for 'Harbour, Bangor' by Colin Middleton, with acknowledgements to Mrs K. Middleton for permission to print.

BRIDGEMAN ART LIBRARY, London, and The Fine Art Society, London, for 'The Dreamers' from 'The Geneva Window' by Harry Clarke, with acknowledgements to Mr D. Clarke for permission to print, and for 'The Eastern Gown' by Sir William Orpen from Atkinson Art Gallery, Southport, Lancs, with acknowledgements to Ms K. Orpen Casey for permission to print.

YONA CAFFREY for 'Couplet'. Reprinted by permission of the artist.

THE CASTLETOWN FOUNDATION, Celbridge, for 'Winter, 1911' by Harriet Hockley Townshend, with acknowledgements to Mdme L. de Douzon for permission to print.

CHRISTIE'S, SCOTLAND LTD, Glasgow, for 'The Limerick Girl' and 'The Playboy' by Sean Keating, with acknowledgements to The Estate of Sean Keating for permission to print; for 'Self-portrait' by John Luke, with acknowledgements to Mrs S. McKee for permission to print; for 'Caravan in Sunlight' by Frank McKelvey, with acknowledgements to Mr R. McKelvey for permission to print; for 'Girl in a Green Sweater' and 'Seated Nude' by Roderic O'Conor, with acknowledgements to Sister Olga Dwyer for permission to print; for 'Girl with Mandolin' by Daniel O'Neill;

for 'Portrait of Mary Potter' by Sir Robert Ponsonby Staples, with acknowledgements to Mrs H. Radclyffe Dolling for permission to print; and for 'Night in a Small Town' by Jack B. Yeats, with acknowledgements to Ms A. Yeats for permission to print.

CHRISTIE'S IMAGES, London, for 'Grace by Candlelight' by Sir William Orpen, with acknowledgements to Ms K. Orpen Casey for permission to print.

CAREY CLARKE PRHA for 'Portrait of the Artist's Mother, Mrs H. E. Clarke'. (1986 36 in. x 30 in.) Reprinted by permission of the artist.

CRAWFORD MUNICIPAL ART GALLERY, Cork, for 'A Female Nude Study', Anonymous; for 'An Samhradh Samh' by Muriel Brandt, with acknowledgements to Ms A. and Mr O. Kane and Ms E. Brandt for permission to print; for 'Wisteria' by Mildred Ann Butler; for 'Market Women' by Hugh Charde; for 'Portrait of John Philpott Curran' by Edward Gribbon; for 'Economic Pressure' by Sean Keating, with acknowledgements to The Estate of Sean Keating for permission to print; for 'The Falconer' by Daniel Maclise; for 'Gathering Kelp' by William Magrath; for 'The Red Rose' by Sir John Lavery, with acknowledgements to Ms J. Donnelly for permission to print; and for 'Lady in White' by Estella Solomons, with acknowledgements to Dr. M. Solomons for permission to print.

FINE ART PHOTOGRAPHIC LIBRARY, London, for 'A Cottage Garden at Sunset' by David Woodlock.

THE GORRY GALLERY, Dublin, for 'Sunlight on the Floor' by Patrick Hennessy, with acknowledgements to the Trustees of Mr H.R. Craig's Will Trust for permission to print; for 'Portrait of Eamon Morrissey' by Edward McGuire, with acknowledgements to Mrs S. McGuire for permission to print; and for 'Daffodils' by William Osborne.

TIM GOULDING for 'In the Realms of Light', 'Out of Darkness 1' and 'Voyage'. Reprinted by permission of the artist with acknowledgements to Jake Sutton for the photography.

HUGH LANE MUNICIPAL GALLERY, Dublin, for 'The Tipperary Hurler' by Sean Keating with acknowledgements to The Estate of Sean Keating; for 'The Unfinished Harmony' and 'Hazel, Lady Lavery at an Easel' by Sir John Lavery, with acknowledgements to Ms J. Donnelly for permission to reprint; for 'The Tinsel Scarf' by William Leech, with acknowledgements to Mrs B.V. Mitchell for permission to print; and for 'A Breezy Day, Howth' and 'Portrait of the Artist's Wife' by Sir William Orpen, with acknowledgements to Ms K. Orpen Casey for permission to print.

IMPERIAL WAR MUSEUM, London, for 'The Refugee' by Sir William Orpen, with acknowledgements to Ms K. Orpen Casey for permission to reprint.

JAMES ADAMS SALEROOMS, Dublin, for 'A Bend in the River Lee' by Cecil Galbally, with acknowledgements to Messrs J. and J. Galbally for permission to print; for 'King O'Toole' by Sean Keating, with acknowledgements to The Estate of Sean Keating for permission to print; and for 'Portrait of the Artist's Sister' by Sir William Orpen, with acknowledgements to Ms K. Orpen Casey for permission to print.

KERLIN GALLERY, Dublin, for 'Ice-Fields' (1990 oil on paper, 18 x 25.5 cm) by Gwen O'Dowd. Reprinted by permission of the artist.

LEEDS MUSEUMS AND GALLERIES (CITY ART GALLERY) for 'Nude Study, 1906' by Sir William Orpen, with acknowledgements to Ms K. Orpen Casey for permission to print.

LISBURN MUSEUM for 'The Bridal Dress' by Samuel McCloy.

NATIONAL GALLERY OF IRELAND, Dublin, for 'Annie Callwell' by Sir Frederick Burton; for 'Molly Macree' by Thomas Jones; for 'The Death of Adonis' by James Barry; and for 'Lovers in a Landscape' by Thomas Bridgeford.

NATIONAL GALLERY OF VICTORIA, Melbourne, Australia, for 'Night' (oil on canvas, 76.5 x 64 cm, Felton Bequest, 1929) by Sir William Orpen, with acknowledgements to Ms K. Orpen Casey for permission to print.

PHILLIPS FINE ART AUCTIONEERS, London, for 'A Garden in France' by Sir John Lavery, with acknowledgements to Ms J. Donnelly for permission to print; for 'Portrait of Miss Jennie Simson' by Sir William Orpen, with acknowledgements to Ms K. Orpen Casey for permission to print; and for 'September Gale' by Jack B. Yeats, with acknowledgements to Ms A. Yeats for permission to print.

SLIGO COUNTY GALLERY, Sligo, for 'A Portrait of Kitsy Franklin' by George Russell (AE), reprinted by the permission of Russell & Volkening as agents for the copyright owner.

SOTHEBYS TRANSPARENCY LIBRARY, London, for 'Man in Red with his Horse' by Hugh Hamilton.

TOWN HOUSE, Dublin, for 'Girl Reading, c. 1910' by Roderic O'Conor, with acknowledgements to Sister Olga Dwyer for permission to print.

ULSTER MUSEUM, Belfast, for 'Summer Evening, Achill' by Micheal J. de Burca, with acknowledgements to Mr A. Bourke for permission to print; 'Coortin'' by William Conor, with acknowledgements to Mrs P. K. Dalzell for permission to print; for 'Strickland's Glen, Bangor' by Samuel McCloy; for 'Man and a Woman' by Norman Morrow; for 'The Red Hammock' by Sir John Lavery, with acknowledgements to Ms J. Donnelly for permission to print; and for 'Resting' by Sir William Orpen, with acknowledgements to Ms K. Orpen Casey for permission to print.

QUEEN'S UNIVERSITY, Belfast, for 'Memory of Les Sylphides' by Sidney Smith, with acknowledgements to Ms P. Chabanais for permission to print.

The editor would like to thank all who helped her with this book, in particular the following people who were generous with their time and encouragement: Pauline Allwright of the Imperial War Museum; Martyn Anglesey, Denise Ferran and Pat McLean of The Ulster Museum; Bruce Arnold; Jonathan Benington; Elaine Campion of Town House; Pamela Coyle, Michael Gill, Deirdre Rennison Kunz and Fergal Tobin of Gill & Macmillan Ltd; Joanna Cramsie of The Castletown Foundation; Professor Anne Crookshank; John de Vere White; Theo Dorgan and the staff of Poetry Ireland; Geoffrey Edwards and Philip Jago of The National Gallery of Victoria; Jean Barry and Peter Fallon of The Gallery Press; David Fitzgerald of The Kerlin Gallery; Elaine Flanigan of Lisburn Museum; Michael Foley of The Art House Register; Liz Forster of The Hugh Lane Municipal Art Gallery; Briona Gleeson and Peter Murray of The Crawford Municipal Art Gallery; Thérèse Gorry of The Gorry Gallery; Eveline Grief of The Royal Hibernian Academy; Josephine Kelliher and Peter McKenna of The Rubicon Gallery; The Knight of Glin; Shirley Lanagan of The Butler Gallery; Adrian Le Harivel and Marie McFeely of The National Gallery of Ireland; Joanna Ling of Sotheby's Transparency Library; Derek Mahon; James O'Halloran of James Adams Salerooms; Maureen Porteous of AIB; Hazel Radclyffe Dolling; Greer Ramsey of Armagh Museum; Anne-Marie Shurey of Phillips Picture Library; Christine Stokes of Leeds Art Gallery; Patrick Taylor of The Taylor Gallery; Donald Tinney of Sligo County Gallery; and Bernard Williams of Christie's Scotland. Special thanks are due to Jill Coote, for the dedication that won her new skills.